MW01242417

Whiskey For The Wounded

Chronicles Of The Resilient Heart

By: J.M. Pozon

Copyright © 2017 J.M Pozon

All rights reserved.

ISBN: 9781521267387

Dedicated to my young kings Isaiah and Noah. I know you won't be able to enjoy this book, just yet. However, this is for the day you become men and outgrow childish fairytales. As you mature, you'll quickly figure out, that this world is anything but easy. But, I hope that when this world tries to tear you down, that you'll meet every challenge with courage and fortitude. Stand unapologetically in who you and be unyielding in pursuit of your goals. Above all else, always believe in yourselves as I believe in you. – Love you forever, until always Mom.

J. M. Pozon

Exordium

Our vices may not be the same, but we're all just looking

for a way to numb the pain.

TABLE OF CONTENTS

Dedication

J. M. Pozon

Section I
The Deceivers

Illusionist

Powerful illusions lead to ominous

Conclusions

Sold me a dream, I purchased

Outright

Little did I know, my soul would be the

purchasing price

It was a hard sell. But, you market

it well

Had me feeling like I was flying

through heaven…

When really I was just burning in the

flames of hell

Eyes wide opened, finally I am awoken,

your spell is broken

Or so I was hoping, seems I am roped in. In the

distance its smoking.

My bridges is burning. Slowly, I am learning.

Discerning truth in your sea of lies,

but the damage is done

What good is a lesson, when learned

too late. None.

J. M. Pozon

Fool's Gold

I look for you in everyone

I meet

Behind the eyes of every man,

I pass by on the streets

Even searched for you in the few lucky men,

That I brought home

Hoping to find you off in some

distant moan

Or somewhere in between satin

bedroom sheets

For, it was there, that you

hypnotized me

Lord knows you always were a special kind

of savage beast

I mean, isn't it tragic, that even the most esteemed women

fall prey to D magic

So here I stand, under the thumb, of hard

D**K and bubble gum

Living life, with all the false fallacies

of you I created

Whiskey For The wounded

Never giving thought to all the things

about you I once hated

My love for you inflated, memories

exaggerated

They're not real, they're

gold plated

Baby, you're Fool's gold,

no value

J. M. Pozon

Naked Amongst The Wolves

Used to say that you worried about me,

hurting you

All the while I should've been more concerned

with you hurting me

This whole time I was the sheep and you were

the lone wolf

Damn….

And, I thought this love was

Kismet

Baby, you were supposed, to be

my safe bet

Guess, somewhere along the way, I forgot to

play those games you play

Seems, I was playing checkers, while you

we're playing chess

Pedestal

Somehow, my wrong doings,

martyred you

Blinded by my own misdeeds, I never took

heed of yours

So I clung to the light in your darkness,

only seeing the best of you

Focused on a single candle in

your abyss

Now, tell me, how did I miss all

your flaws

Glorifying you, from the top of your head

Down to your dirty drawls

Seems somewhere, along the way; I put you high up

on that pedestal

And, I forgot to take you down

J. M. Pozon

Hidden Agendas

There's no such thing as

friendly devils

People always have angles and

hidden agendas

So better learn to keep your

head on a swivel

Plastic People

I kept looking for real,

in fake people

Searching for depth in

shallow places.

Finding love in all the

wrong places

J. M. Pozon

Devil has a face

Sweet talking

charmer

Silver tongued

snake

If only I would've

known

I would have ran from

my mistakes

A nightmare in

Disguise

A beautiful dream

wrapped in lies

The devil has a face and it looks

 a lot like yours

Whiskey For The wounded

Three Times A Fool

They say fool me once, shame

on you

Fool me twice and its shame

on me

But, fool me three times and I am a

*motherf***ing fool*

Guess the jokes

on me

What's worse is I still can't

let you be

Lately, it seems, I've been in a constant tug a war, between me,

you and my dignity

And dignity is losing

J. M. Pozon

Uncut Grass

Slippery, slithering

Snake

I've made a grave

mistake

By the time I heard you hissing, your fangs

were piercing skin

You wrapped around

my throat

Soon I began to choke

Now, I am slipping really fast. All because I

forgot to cut the grass

Beyond The Looking Glass

Beyond the looking glass, I saw a man who

wore a mask

It shielded his face and hid his eyes. An eerie and

chilling disguise

He spoke with seven tongues. And, on the tip of

everyone stood a lie

Both his hands held

destruction

Said this fate was one of my own

construction

I asked to know his meaning, but he just smiled,

handing me a sharpened knife

Staring me in the eye, he told me tonight would

be the night, I died

Startled by his reply, I stabbed him twice in his side. As he fell,

his mask began to slip

And, it was then that I caught a glimpse at the man

behind the looking glass

Only to see that He was me…

J. M. Pozon

I'll take that bet

I see your demons and I raise you,

my devils

Keep Your wool, Fool

Born, veil over eyes, my intuition

never lies

Like a voice screaming in my head, I can literally

hear every time you lie

J. M. Pozon

Opened Tabs

Ordering off the good credit of your

looks and charm

You take and take but give nada

in return

Withdraw after withdraw

but no deposits

But, the bill is due and someone

has to pay the check

Warnings

Blaring are those voices inside your head,

still you shut them down

Writing off that sickening feeling in your gut

as misguided distrust

But, what you think is paranoia is really

just your intuition kicking in

J. M. Pozon

Succubus

She was a pretty little lie, hiding an

ugly truth

Her smile so sweet, but if only

you knew

Behind her eyes,

Lies deceit

Taking men from their feet to

their knees

The source of tears, nightmare

and fears

Over the years, she has laid with many men,

killing them all slowly

over time

Oh so many have fall victim,

to her crimes

And…

Through the heated touches and heaved breaths,

she brings death

Slip of the Mask

You can only hide who you are

for so long.

Sooner or later the real you will

bleed through

See, the devil is vain and sooner or later he'll

want credit for your pain

J. M. Pozon

Rolling Stone

She was the embodiment of all

men's fears

Falling in and out of love every

time the wind blows

Ruthless and cold

No soul, but the red soles on her

Louboutin heels

Dear Ego

Dear ego, I think it's time we

parted ways

I've grown too wise to ever let

you stay

But, I must admit, we had some

good days

See, when I was younger,

I needed you

Needed your hubris and false

confidence

I was still building

my self-esteem

So I feed off you out of

necessity

Now that I am all grown up, I have no

need for such things

J. M. Pozon

Section II
The Grievers

Favorite Lullaby

Two shots of whiskey to chase

my demons away

Add, a little chaser hoping

my angels will stay

J. M. Pozon

Paper Wings

It was just one of those whiskey numbing

cocaine nights

Paper wings gave

her flight

So she soared the sky on

cocaine clouds

Smoking away her life inside of a little

glass pipe

But, that needle in her skin, never seemed to

take away her sins

So she jumped from her paper plane, holding a spoon

to the flame

Soaring high, she climbed up onto hotel

Balconys

She looked up to the sky and leaped believing

she could fly

Nostalgia

Time does funny things

to memories

It makes the past seem

sweeter

And the pain cut deeper

J. M. Pozon

Bottom Of the bottle

I tried to drink to drown

my sorrows

Instead, my sorrows

drowned me

In a sea of alcohol while they

all swam free

Whiskey For The wounded

Shattered

I am just a sum of all my missing pieces and

damaged parts

No! There's no mending my

broken heart

I can't be fixed with glue

or tape

No, this pain, I can't

escape

Got a hole in my soul that

can't be filled

An ache in my chest that can't

be healed

Yet and still, I am giving you all

my shattered pieces

Now, what will you do

with them?

Will you try to put me back

together again?

Or will you cut yourself on all

my ragged edges?

J. M. Pozon

Before the dawn

They tell me, it's always darkest

before the dawn

But, why do the darkest nights always

seem to last so long?

And, yea I know the morning

sun will come

Still… in that dead silence of my

darkest nights

I find myself longing for the warmth of

the suns rays

Whiskey For The wounded

Rearview

Here's the thing about rearview
mirrors
If you keep looking back while
trying to move forward eventually
you crash

J. M. Pozon

Buried Alive

The hurts too heavy to carry,

so you try to bury it

But, the pain

is you

To bury it, you must bury parts

of yourself too

So now, you've been

buried alive

Walking around, a shell of

your former self

Lying Whispers

The Mirror lies, telling her she's not

thin enough

The refrigerator lies, saying it can take

the pain away

And, the toilet hides all the evidence

That she provides

Two fingers inside her mouth, as she tries to

Fight to make it all go away

J. M. Pozon

Storms Overhead

Dark Clouds are looming

Overhead.

A quiet storm, silently brewing while

he lays in bed

Words, never spoken

or said.

Now being pushed onto paper through

pencil and lead.

Listen closely and you can hear the screams inside

this silent mans head

The voices are whispers of the dead,

welcoming a new friend

Whiskey For The wounded

Return to Sender

On cold hard metal I lay, under bright

fluorescent lights

Deep down, in my soul I known that this

Just ain't right

Can this really be worth the pain? Or the stain

it will leave on my soul?

But, for a single mother with

two kids already

The task just seems too heavy

for going it alone

So I play god, deciding to terminate sealing an

unborn child's fate

Hope the lord forgives me, for committing such

a monstrous act…

God sent me a gift. And shamefully

I sent it back

J. M. Pozon

The Candy Is Rotten

He gave her

candy

He gave her

sweets

Then he lightly kissed her

cheeks

Shhh … he whispered, one hand

Over mouth

The other resting on her

tiny little knee

The Cutter

The pain was silent until she gave

it a voice

Now it sings freely as silver shines

on deeply pierced skin

Red lines, mirroring the pain buried

deep within

J. M. Pozon

Uninvited Guest

Misery and all its company took a seat

at my dinner table

They ate all my food and drank up

all my wine

Man slaughter

She live in fear of high school

hallways

Walking on eggshells, longing for the

mercies of first bells

Daily, she's teased and Mocked, Butt end

of all their jokes

To them, it's just fun, games and

harmless play.

But, she doesn't feel quite

the same way

In fact, she no longer feel at all

Numb…

As they laugh and shove past her, she hears

one of them call her whore.

Staring down at dropped books, she can

take no more

And, so she begins thinking of ways to

end it all .

J. M. Pozon

Grief

You're entire world just

stopped

But the world around you

kept spinning

Now to be fair, it's not that they

don't care

However for them the sadness

is brief

So you stand alone in this ocean

of grief

They try, but can't really understand the

emptiness or loss

Or feel the pieces of you that are now

forever lost

The world has moved on and before long you'll

have to learn to do the same

So in the midst of your pain, force yourself

out bed each and every day.

And, keep feigning smiles until the day they

becomes real

Two pink lines

I can still remember the day, I first saw those

two pink lines.

I was elated….

But then, baby showers, turned to condolence

cards and sympathy flowers

Can I still call myself a parent, if I've never

seen your face?

Doctors say I can try it

again

As if you're something that can

just be replaced

Empty painted nurseries now

torture me

Haunted by memories of what

will never be

And, now when I open scrapbooks to stare at

those two pink lines

I simply break down and cry

J. M. Pozon

One Day

The pain never really

goes away

But, one day it won't cut

so deeply

The Wolves Within

Bereaved whispers echo into the

chilled winds

As regrets scent rises off ocean

waves

Contrite howls of woe at the break

Of day?

Wolves give chase through the

moonlight

They corner me, but they

don't bite

Even they know that this here is really a

Internal fight

J. M. Pozon

Section III
The Sleepers

Red or Blue Pill

Eyes wide opened, but you're still

sleeping

Mindless cattle

They give you drugs to fry

your brains

Yet, you smile at your enslavers and thank

them for your chains

Willing believers, following blindly behind

the deceivers of men

Asleep in a cloud of purple haze that keeps you

in a compliant daze

All the while, they murder our brothers and fathers

Like pigs to the slaughter

And, for those who are awakened, their lives are

quickly taken

We all know, just how dangerous it is to be right,

when the government is wrong

J. M. Pozon

Sleeping on yourself

Sometimes, you are the reason you

haven't made it yet.

Spent more on the bed than you

did on the dream

Children Shouldn't Play
With Dead Things

This is for the living

undead

Breathing talking zombies, sleep walking

through life

The ones who can't go a single day without

a fix to get them by

Stoned

High as a kite as they let life pass

them by

No ambitions or life

longs plans

Just zombies in a drug

induced trance

Distant from reality, paranoia and

delusions are grand

And, every failed drug test is just part of the

man's evil plan

Now they're jobless, spending money they don't have,

on a habit they can't afford

But still it's Puff, puff pass....

J. M. Pozon

Good Intentions

The gates to hell is held opened by

people who mean well

Whiskey For The wounded

Mental Prisons

Caged in, but this prison, is one built,

from my own sins

J. M. Pozon

Hamster Wheel

I am stuck in the

rat race

Cat chases rat and rat

chases cheese

But neither eats…

The wheels just keeps

spinning

But, just surviving ain't

living

Still, round and round

it goes…

We spend our whole life

chasing checks

Working to make rich

man richer

Go figure, we punch these clocks for that

time and a half

But this day to day to grind, is slowly chipping away at

our vitality

Shits draining, exchanging vital life energy for goals

not worth attaining

Whiskey For The wounded

Bumps in the night

I don't know what's more

frightening

These monsters underneath

my bed

Or those skeletons in your closet

J. M. Pozon

Broken Clocks

Tick tock, Tick tock

time stops

My thoughts

stand still

It gets a little hard, trying to decipher

what's really real

Swear, sometimes it's like I am

frozen in time.

Lost somewhere, inside my

own mind

Section IV
The Dreamers

J. M. Pozon

Manifest Destiny

Soft giggles…. Hushed

whispers

Just look at them, praying on

my downfall

But, they laugh because they can't

see my vision

And, I laugh because I know they can't change what's

already been written

Baby success is in bones and this shit

is written in stone

There's no

stopping me

Guess, you can call this manifest

destiny

Hubris

Think God knows, that every now and then,

I need to stumble

Somehow, my missteps keep me

humble

J. M. Pozon

Lucid Dreaming

Late at night, I close

my eyes

I try to convince myself that

reality is wrong

And, my dreams are real

Victory Laps

I am focused, determined,

ready to win.

The critics won't ever doubt

me again.

Darkness is gone, I am ready

to shine.

It's Victory Time.

J. M. Pozon

Growing Pains

Shedding superficial pleasures in search

 of something better

In reflection, I am starving for more

profound connections

But, it's hard when your friends are still

on that same shit

Out there every weekend, parting, bar hoping

bottle popping

Feels like we've got nothing in common,

young minded, short sided

Never evolving…

And, every time I try to pull them out them

out their mental limitation

 It only ends in further

frustration

No doubt about it, hardest thing

I ever had to do was to out grow the ones

I cared about

Whiskey For The wounded

Gone With the Wind

Keep reaching for success until it

reaches back

Only way to outrun failure is to keep

running laps

J. M. Pozon

Serendipity

Heartache can be a catalyst

for greatness

Inspiration fueled by heartbreak, often ignites a

sort of creative genius

So don't run from the pain,

run towards it

And, let it inspire you

This House you Built

You've made fear and complacency

your landlord

You keep paying rent

to doubts

But you can't negotiate with

poverty

J. M. Pozon

Dreamland

The place where infeasible

fallacies

Are transformed into infinite

realities

Whiskey For The wounded

Street Smarts

That's the thing about

Intuition

It sees, that which is

hidden

That, which can't be solved by

books or college

It sees the kind of shit, that's invisible to the

eyes of logic

I Wonder

Sometimes I wonder...

What would happen, if one day, I awoke to all my

dreams come true

Would I still be me?

Or would I switch it up and

change

Masters of Fate

The universe won't believe

if you don't

The first step in receiving a blessing is

believing you deserve it

Mindset is paramount to everything you

want to achieve

J. M. Pozon

Jakie Boy

Said I was jack of

all trades

But that something ole

timers say

In truth, I used to have

Jake shit …

So I traded in jack, to become a slave to

an enslaver of trades

Slayed my enslaver, now I am a master

to them all

Glass Ceilings

Bump, the hype. Success is

up to you

You decide whether or not

you make it

See that ceilings only glass, until you `

fucking break it

J. M. Pozon

Rude Awakenings

I looked up to the sky and

whispered softly...

I said Lord, they're sleeping

on me

To which he replied, its okay there's a reward

deep within your Hunger

So let them sleep a little while longer, I've already

set the alarm clock

Whiskey For The wounded

Premonitions Of Greatness

I visited the future and took a glimpse at my

past and saw my present

Future me, spoke to the present me, saying that this

would be my life's defining moment

So, whatever you do make sure you take hold

of it and own it

To which, I replied, no worries, I got you,

I am on it

J. M. Pozon

Blood, Sweat, and Tears

Man I am working, pockets hurting

family ain't supporting

Spent year after year, draft after draft

perfecting my craft

Still, they don't see my struggle,

don't peep the hustle

But, what they don't understand is that

failure is not an option…

See, I want this as much as

I want to breathe

So give me success or just give

me death

Cus I am ready for whatever comes first or

whatever comes next

Dreamers

Not everyone will believe

in you

So called friends will mock you, while secretly

hoping that you fail

Even members of your own family will

try to hinder and derail

And, when you do succeed, there will be those that

still who won't give you credit for all

you've achieved

I say that to say, sometimes you just gotta

do it for you

J. M. Pozon

Feasible

I told God, I don't need to

be easy.

I just need it to be

possible.

Whiskey For The wounded

Grand Delusions

It is unspoken truth, that the quest for greatness

is a lonely pursuit

See, heightened ambitions, make mediocre

minds uncomfortable

Many will define your dreams as unpractical

Delusions …

But, truth is you're simply reacting to a vision

they cannot see

However, success most often comes to those who are

absolutely obsessed with it

So revel in your most absurd and grandest

delusions of it

J. M. Pozon

Keep that Energy

Nah, son. Keep that same energy cus

I aint the one

See, I reached out to the

 Lot of you

Only to have my hands

smacked down

 I aint forget. And, in the end, what you give is

what you get

Pretty Savages

She's about her

business

Takes what's hers and never ask

for forgiveness

She living, no

fucks given

Critics talking but she ain't

listening

She gets high on

Success

Gets, off on making it on her own

Self-made Woman

Ain't out here looking for

no meal tickets

She owns her kitchen and she's doing

all the cooking

Her own sponsor. Living lavish. Such a pretty

fucking savage

J. M. Pozon

Cost of ambition

You'll have no social life and there'll be

lots of sleepless nights

On top of that, you're ambition

is probably going to cost you a

couple friends

And, the hours you put in will be the same reason

some of your relationships will end

Resilience

I work as it my talents weren't

God given

So I'll never apologize for my

ambition

I don't believe in

quitting

There's only one word to

describe me driven

J. M. Pozon

Sparks

Lost, aimlessly wandering, not sure of

which way to go

But, in time you'll find, that one thing that

Ignites your soul

It only takes a tiny spark to

set a fire

Starving Artist

So hungry for success, my belly's aching,

call those hunger pains

They told me quit, get a real job, but this

hustle it's in my veins

Late nights, early mornings…

I'll put in eighty so I don't ever have to

work a forty

J. M. Pozon

Come Back King

I understand being

down and out

Hell, I've been there more times

than I can count

But, what I can't understand, is anyone being

willing to stay there

Your Story

You are the author of

your Life

Can't be bitter about a story

That you wrote

At any time, you can change the

narrative

J. M. Pozon

Master Plans

There's a million fucking ways to

get it. Choose one

And, then choose

another one

Whiskey For The wounded

Changing reflections

If one day you wake and find, you don't like the person
you've become... Change it...
Reinvent yourself as many times as it takes until your
satisfied with who you are.
Because, behind that self-reflecting mirror, there's a greater version
of yourself waiting to break through

J. M. Pozon

Band wagon

They're jealous of you. Secretly hating but they

smile and they fake it

Screaming, that they knew all along that

you'd make it

Success brings

them out

Showing fake love with their

hands out

Bandwagon friends, but then

again

Each new level has
its devils

Washed Up

Who would've thought you'd

make it this far

Standing in that

limelight

Sold out shows each and

every night

It's a high of the highest kind,

no narcotics

But, that fame

is fickle

How quickly the glory fades, you outlived

your glory days

No longer, a household

name

 The fame has moved on to

someone new

Now you're just a

has been

Chasing a feeling, you'll never

feel again.

J. M. Pozon

What If ?

What if's turn reality if you don't

catch them in time

So, I stay on my grind, overlooking nothing,

leaving nothing behind

Sluggard

Don't, unknowing be the guy who sleeps

his way into poverty

See, complacency leads to
mediocracy

And, mediocracy leads to

disappointment

J. M. Pozon

Tend To Your Gardens

Realize it or not, we are always creating

our own realities

So be conscientious of what

seeds you plant

Your future depends on what you allow to grow

in your subconscious mind

Loaded Guns

Loaded guns, eventually

shoot

So don't wait for last straws or

pulled triggers

J. M. Pozon

Catalyzing Agents

This is for the nineth grade teacher

who told me ...

"That I wouldn't won't get far in life and might as well get use

to bagging groceries"

This is the Ex's who played into my fears of

not being good enough

This is for my ex husband, who convinced me that

no one else would want me

This is for my mother who taught me to never

take no as an answer.

And, to build my own doors and

walk through them

For my father who taught me humility and how

to be humble

This is for Ms. Heiss... The humanities teacher who made

fall in love learning.

As she, feed my fascination of

philosophy and greek mythology

This is for my basketball coach, who pushed me further than

I'd ever thought I could go

More importantly, this is for

Whiskey For The wounded

Isaiah and Noah

You're the reason behind why I could

never give up

Good or bad, you're all the

reason I am here

J. M. Pozon

Section V
The Lovers

Worth Saving

You're persistently pursuing, but I tell you

no blatantly

Yet you're still contemplating

saving me

Too much of a realist to pretend that I don't

know how this story ends

It wouldn't be fair to let u stay, so I am constantly

pushing you away

Not, that I don't want you,

because I do

But, in truth, I've got nothing but the worst

of me to give to you

See my ex took the best of me, therefore you can only get

what is left of me

And, yea I know u hear what they

say of me

But, I am not exactly the way they're

painting me

Still, life experiences have surely

tainted me

Now you're mentally debating the risk Still, you

J. M. Pozon

want to persist,

But loving me is like aiming at a target

that you'll always miss

Like being homesick for a place that

doesn't exists

So in reality, we'd never really be together,

sort of just coexist

Okay, let's just say we did manage, I've been

so badly damaged

Cold distant and bitter, no emotional filter

No fixing me magically

Tragically soul filled with calamity, but I do

have a heart

Shit just beats ... real slow. And, so I'm constantly

putting up walls

Top it all off, I am no good at showing

affection at all

Another one of pains manifestations, keep my emotions,

buried deep inside

Call it foolish, woman's pride. Strong Independent, driven,

still something is missing.

Coincidence, it feels like my soul just wasn't

meant for this

So I use work to substitute

Whiskey For The wounded

the emptiness

Turning, pain to blind

ambition

Success makes me

feel better

So I enjoy the momentary highs as I accomplish

my endeavors

You call it irony, I call it fate. My pains my

motivation

In relation, if I wasn't so fucked up, I probably

wouldn't be as great

The pain is a part of me, take it away, you take away

damn near all of me

Now, you're a man, so you'll try to understand

what I been through

But, my pain much too deeply rooted

for you to attend too

And plus, as if that wasn't enough, got a really

bad issue with trust

Can't deny thou, sometimes I look in your eyes,

I get lost in them

I get to feeling like there's might be a

little bit of hope

J. M. Pozon

But, then nope. Feeling quickly replaced

Anger hit my face

Enraged by the fact you got to fix what that

man broke

And, yeah I know at some point, I have to

learn to love again

But at this point, I'm so fucking straight on love,

I ain't never trying love again

Tell you the brutal truth, because when it end

badly I don't want you blaming me.

So I'll just leave it up you to decide if it's really

worth saving me

Whiskey For The wounded

In The Wind

Suddenly, everything is different

we drifting

 I can feel the shift in

your attention

Slowly, but surely I am

losing you

And, what am I to do? I invested so much of

myself into this relationship

It kind of feels like I am

losing me too

J. M. Pozon

Worn out Welcomes

There's been too many goodbyes,

to care for your hellos

Too many times that I've begged you

 not to go

Desensitize, out of cries. No more

Strength left to try

Never, Neverland

Heartbreaks and heart

aches

Still, I keep searching for

neverland

But, I feel like I am flying and I'll

never land

J. M. Pozon

Things We Lost In The Fire

Somewhere, along the way…..

We lost one of the greatest aspects

of our feminity

Pain, struggle and grief, deprieved us of our

ability to be submissive

For so many years were taught to

distrust you

In return, you learned not to trust

you either

So fear of failure, makes you run away from

Your responsibilityies of being a husband

or a father

Left alone to carry the load, so we harbor these

intense feelings of resement

And, by the time that the next man comes around,

we are leery of his commitment

Life experience has shown us that the only ones we can

depend on is us

And, thus we go through life unable to wholeheartedly

trust in our men

Whiskey For The wounded

Bitter Sweet

I know, I can be a

headache

But, trust me, I make up

for it

Especially in between

those sheets

See without the bitter, sweet just

ain't as sweet

J. M. Pozon

Life Support

What we lost, we can't ever

get it back

See the floodgates opened and

the dam gave way

Slowly, I am starting to

 pull away,

All while hoping, that you'd fight

to make me stay

But, pride gets in the way, so instead,

you give me space

Now there's a thousand worlds

between you and I

Can you feel the distance?

I can

And, it's the furthest away from you,

I've ever felt…

It's like you're floating in

outer space

Somewhere out there on

Orion's belt

Whiskey For The wounded

But, this can't be

how it ends

Our love blowing away in the

intergalactic winds

So I am crying out to you with

my silence

And it's the loudest I've

ever been

Love is dying, but frankly, I am

done trying to revive us

So I give a tug on the plug and flat line us...

J. M. Pozon

Make believe

You are every fairy tale

come to life

Fiction made

Flesh

Heartbreak laid

to rest

Whiskey For The wounded

Johnny Appleseed ??

What happened to always

and forever?

Guess forever is shorter for

some people

I think the worst part is saying good bye to that life you

envisioned inside your mind

Still think our daughter Catalina, would've

been one of a kind

Some days, I long for the simple things I never

got to experience

Like thanksgiving dinners with

your family

Or learning the recipe to your aunt Carols

chessy baked potatoes

But, truth is nothing last forever,

not even us.

J. M. Pozon

Don't Track Mud In
The House

Don't you dare track mud across my heart

with dirty shoes

Or touch my soul with your

unclean hands

Don't tread on me and I won't

tread on you

Self-Sabotage

You tell me, this is the real deal, still I can't
Allow myself to believe it
You give me your love, but I don't know to permit
Myself to receive it
Still, you give me all you have to give and
I can't conceive it
All I can think is, what if I invest in you and get no
return on my investment

Your effort and loyalty is there and it's not that
I don't see it
But the thing is, to accept your spoken truth? Then I'd
have to admit to myself
That there's something worth
loving in me
And well, loving one's self is afar more
difficult feat

J. M. Pozon

A Thousand Picasso's

Hurt an artist and you'll forever

Be their muse

Hurt a poet and you'll be remembered

throughout history

Whiskey For The wounded

This immortal
love

When love died, I buried it six feet deep

beneath soft earth

But, as it seems, buried love, keeps rising

from grave

Breathing life into these old ashes; I once

laid to rest

J. M. Pozon

Old Flames

Trust me nothing

Changed

That old flame still burns

the same

I know the heat of their passion still warms you,

but let me warn you

While it feels nice, going back, only gets you

burned twice

Ships in the night

I thought our love would be the greatest

story ever written

Instead, A horror story is what

was given.

Now we're living life like two

distant strangers

Just passing each other by like ships

in the night

J. M. Pozon

Kindred Spirits

Swear, it's like we

met before

Energy is on point as well as

the vibe

Kindred spirits of the

same kind

Whiskey For The wounded

Guarded

How can you ever expect to fall in

love again?

When those walls built to keep pain out, also keep

all your love caged in

J. M. Pozon

Revolving Doors

Hmmm….. you do know that revolving doors,

go both ways

You keep telling him to leave but then

letting him stay

Pay the Toll

"Wisdom is a gift and its currency is pain"

J. M. Pozon

Exit Strategies

Knowing when to walk away is as vital to

survival as drawing breath

See loving the wrong person, too long is the

Equivalent to a slow death

Caged Bird

Caged bird under water,

Drowing at sea

Spent its whole life walking on egg shells

dying to be free

J. M. Pozon

Fickle Man

Don't you dare play with someone

else's feelings

Simply because you're unsure of

your own

Rekindled

There should be urgency

in your desires

Only way to create a spark

is with fire

J. M. Pozon

Blame Game

They say you can't run from

the pain

So where do you point those

fingers when there's no one

to blame?

Eye of the Beholder

They said, we were broken and

wouldn't last

But, I've never see anything more

beautiful than a sunset through

broken glass

J. M. Pozon

Knock Offs

Love is constant. Lust its

fickle substitute

Whiskey For The wounded

Prince Charming Is
A Fraud

I've been robbed. I kissed an

enchanted frog

But, all I got was a pretty little heartthrob,

with no heartbeat

Bamboozled and tricked, given mere

bones for kings' meat

Still, how could I see, what cunning ruse

lurked underneath.

He played his part well; even had me

believing in fairytales

But then the hourglass fell and the clock stroke

twelve and all was revealed.

J. M. Pozon

"I Love You"

Not every I love is

the same

Some are filled with joy, while others

are filled with pain

Others just a line feed, whispered

by a lame

Limbo

Stuck somewhere between, I fucking hate

you so much

And, I can't fucking breathe

without you

J. M. Pozon

Embody Me

I want that special spiritual kind

of connection

The kind that when I look at you, it's sort of like

staring at my own reflection

Whiskey For The wounded

Bird in the bush

I am tired of always being the one

who got away

Just once, I want someone to appreciate me

while they've got me

J. M. Pozon

Safe Haven

You're my safe haven, a safe place,

for me to land

Never afraid, because I know I am

in safe hands

With you, I always know exactly

where I stand

And, when I go adrift, your love give me the

strength to dive off cliffs

Even in the dark, you give me courage to swim

with sharks

Quick Sand

Your love keeps pulling

me deep

The more I struggle, the faster

I sink

And, before I know it, I am neck deep

in quicksand

J. M. Pozon

Wild Fires

Some people are

wild fires

Scorching everything in

their paths

Leaving destruction in

their wake

They'll set your soul on fire and leave

you burning in the flames

Safety Net

Like a fool I fell

for you

Thankfully, my dignity broke

the fall

J. M. Pozon

Rose Colored Glasses

The more I tried to see

the good in you

The more determined you became

with hiding it

Place Holders

You never really missed them, just the feelings

of warm beds and laughter shared

Of coming home and having

someone there

Sharing your day with someone

who cares

But, really you're just two people

breathing the same air

Deep down, you know the connection

isn't really there

The vibe is all wrong and even when you're together it

still feels like no ones there

J. M. Pozon

Damn, those eyes...

I see magic

in you

Drawn to you like the ocean

to the moon

Whiskey For The wounded

Section VI
How the world
Ends

Spoils of War

Up upon the mountain top

I stand

Staring out, over the horizons at a loveless

land of soulless men

I sit and watch as children weep in

desert heat.

As planes fly by, raining death on foreign streets

I feel my heart skip a beat

As I think of tortured screams, corruption greed and

forgotten liberties

The sacrifice of war is always death and it cares not

which side provides

So blood spills and in reply, soldiers die, fighting

battles purchased by lies

And, when its all said and done, all that's left is metal casings,

dog tags and folded flags

Whiskey For The wounded

Good bye World

This is the way the world ends, with senseless

killing of innocent men

This is the way

world dies

One forgotten child

at time

This is the way the world cries, with the tears of

orphans and widowed wives

This is the way world fades desensitizing us

each and every day

Can you feel them? Slowly, stripping away,

all of our humanity

And, this is the way it will go until we have forgotten,

the value of human life

J. M. Pozon

At Midnight We Eat

Suffering, poverty, famine

Illness and disease

With tear filled eyes they cry

On bended knees

Skin stuck to ribs, starving kids

who barely breathe

In late night silence, you can hear their

anguished screams

Midnight nears and in their sleep

they find relief

Hollow Men

Pitiless, soulless creatures, with blackened eyes

And nefarious features

Empty hollow men they are, hearts of rock

that's black as tar

They may be made of flesh bone, but I tell you

now they have no souls

J. M. Pozon

Battle Scars

Empty dreams! And vacant
slumbers
Pulled my ticket, but didn't to punch
my number
They sent me home round
mid-November…
With a head full of memories I'd
Never forget.
Things seen, that could never
be un-seen
Like little girls, with bombs strapped to their chest,
Walking toward Humvees
There are some things that they leave out when you
join the army
Like this little rippling effect called PTSD

Whiskey For The wounded

Section VII
The 25th Hour

American Castaway's

Castaways on a land that's
not our own

We live here but can we realqly call

it home?

We can pledge allegiance to their flag but

we'll never truly be free

Don't believe me then I dare one of you negros

to take a knee

For these are chains around our necks that

you can not see

Systemic racism, mass incarceration, I mean when has

the law ever been on our side?

Because when a black men dies, the whole damn

constitution seems to get revised.

And, these days police brutality is the

new genocide

They say follow the law and abide, but say nothing

when we do just that and still die

I mean come on we can die bed, while

Asleep in our home

But, I guess justice is for everyone, you just better

read between them lines

Terms and condition may apply

Whiskey For The wounded

In Loving Memory

Theres no in loving
memory
For those of us killed by
their hands
They always seem to want and
try to kill us twice
Almost like its not enough to just
take our lives.
Before families can grief or honor
their slained
They already started their slander
campaigns
Assassinating character and defaming
our dead
Before last rites can even
be read
They vilify the victims and humanize
the killers
Dredging up whatever dirt they
can find
As means of justifying their crimes

J. M. Pozon

Grand Rising

Part One

Wheres the call to

action ???

We wear the shirts, we make

the hash tags

And we'll get mad for a

week or two

 Until some celebrity post

 something trival

We'll burn down building and

 tear shit up

Retaliating with all sorts of

petty crimes

But just Imagine if we actually got angry

enough to get organized

See we Mad But we're not

Enraged

And, until we our we'll never be

able to operate

or move on the same page

Grand Rising

Part Two

I've been waiting, waiting for

you to get angry

Ohhhh, there it is . That right There

Can you feel it?

That fire in your eyes, that anger you

feel inside

Everytime another one

of us dies

That's whats needed. See the revolution is near

And, this aint the time for tears

Four hundred year, we've knocked at

that door

No more…. We are tired We are tried and its twelve

past noon on a high tide

So there wont be anymore knocking

of doors Of that I am sure .

In fact, its looking like a mighty fine time to

knock that motherfucker down

J. M. Pozon

Acessory to Murder

You may not have pulled

any triggers

But, you watch in silence as they

murder us

Shooting down my brethren like dogs

in the streets

Still you do not speak, remaining silent

Impartial to these travesties

However, your impartiality is not innocuous,

in fact it makes complicit

An accomplice

A willing participant of all that's wrongs

being comitted

Karen

Racism is your

sword

But, your actions cannot

go ignored

You wear your whiteness like a

cloak of invincibility

Weaponizing your privilege, wielding

it like a knife

You connivie, and deliberately

you lie

Knowing one false cry could cost a

Black Man his life

But know these Karen, you bets keep

yourself in check

Because your white fragility is under no threat

at least not yet

J. M. Pozon

The Reckoning

Martin had a

dream

Malcom had a

vison

And, by the time

we finished

You gonna wish like hell

you listened

Whiskey For The wounded

American Dreaming

American dreams lay shattered

in the slums of the streets

While homeless vets rummage through

trash cans for bites to eat

Its survival of the fittest and your

odds are bleak

See we live in a land where racist old men use stand your ground

laws as their cop-out defense.

Because we all know that being black in America

is the real capital offense.

Out here, it's safer to fight in Iraq, than to have

a run in with a trigger happy cops.

Cheers! Cheers!!!

Here's to our great melting pot. The land of acceptance and

equal opportunity.

The country where immigrants work their entire

life to pay off a mortgage

Only to turn around and be deported.

But, who's to blame…

When tyrants become leaders through

money and fame.

J. M. Pozon

Liberty is bleeding. And, our country's

Is in pain

Still the privilege exploit racial tensions

for beneficial gains

Welcome to America, Land of milk and honey,

and golden opportunity

Whiskey For The wounded

Make America Great Again

As a black woman, it makes
me wonder…
Just what is your definition
of great
Us conforming & falling
in Line
Or perhaps you wish to send
us back in time

J. M. Pozon

Black PTSD

When you see how worthless

we are in their eyes

And, with impunity, how quickly they can

take our lives

How can we not be

Traumatized?

Whiskey For The wounded

Section VII
A Queen Dethroned

EXCERPTS FROM MY BOOK

STAR DUST

J. M. Pozon

Melanin Thief

You're beautiful and don't even

know it

Society takes hold of your beauty and

won't let you own it.

So you look in the mirror and

despise what you see

Because it's not blond hair or blue eyes

you saw on MTV.

You're image of beauty

distorted

Under a mental hold of definitions

of beauty told that dates back to

Centuries old.

Whiskey For The wounded

Little Girl Lost

Maybe it was that one hug daddy

forgot to give

That "I love you" He meant to say;

but she never got to hear

Whatever the case, up she grew looking for that

love that she never knew

From one man to the next looking

for the one who'd treat her like she

was more than sex

Until one day, she met this cat named Terry

Friends called him Rex

But he was spiritually bankrupt burned

shorty's soul up

Turned her out, misusing her body like

a sexual toilet

Her body became his, she no longer

owned it

And, this is the story of little girl lost

J. M. Pozon

Fall from Grace

Where have thy gone my beautiful

sisters of virtue

Oh, how you've let this world delude

and pervert you

Trading in chasten integrity for attention and

honorable mentions

Gaining fame and wealth by exploiting

oneself

Born queens, yet you behave like tools

for their amusement

A complicit generation of willing

"Sarah Baartman's"

Never did think, I'd live to see the day where we allowed empty

vanities to overthrow our morality

We've become so much less than what we

were meant to be

Let's stop being bad bitches and let's go back to

being Queens

Appropriation

You took pieces of me and threw back the

parts me of you hated

I felt jaded….

You'll enjoy in our culture, but won't share

in our pains

Now this isn't me trying to play the

blame game

But understand this, we were made to feel ashamed,

of things like our skin, our hair, our curves and

our names.

So yes….

I get a little confused when they give you credit

which is not due.

Now we all know it's true… even if the message is

cryptic and hidden

They'll praise black features just as long as they're

not on a black woman

J. M. Pozon

The Cycle

Mother and daughter, both one in

the same.

Two generations of women living the

same life twice

Both, of them in love with men that will

never call them wife

A generational curse…

Cycle after cycle of women whom never

learned to put themselves first.

Whiskey For The wounded

Deflowered

An exotic rose, but you've been

deflowered

With Sweet whispers and lying kisses

he stole your power

Busy, busy little bee. He claimed your nectar

and took your honey

J. M. Pozon

Missing Crowned Jewels

You thought, you finally found

your king

A man worthy of the throne you

offered him

So, you invited him into your

sacred palace

Let him drink from the sacred

chalice

But, his intent rested in deceit

and malice

He indulged in the

king spoils

Wore the king's crown, but had no intent

of doubling down

With a mouth full of

gluttony

He took, pillaged and

plundered

Stole everything, even removed the jewels

from your crown.

Whiskey For The wounded

Section VIII
A Throne Reclaimed

Queens Unite

Queens, should never apologize for

being Queens

Your crown.. Your throne. They are your

birthright

Claim it !!

Let Him Go!!

If he walks out your life, your heart

won't stop beating

After everything you been through.

You're still breathing

So trust me when I say, that you don't

need him

Giving Hearts

It's okay to give, just don't give to the

point you have nothing left

Eternal beauty

Be the kind of beautiful that

cannot fade

J. M. Pozon

Irony

He didn't think you were a good

Woman...

Well, not until he tried to find

a better one

Funny, how that works

Labels

Hoe… Slut… Whore….

How, you've fallen victim to those labels

they gave you

But these names don't reflect

who you truly are

Those titles couldn't be anything

further from the truth

Don't let the arbitrary opinions of others neuter

or subdue you

You are and will always be what you believe

yourself to be

So, in truth only you can save you

J. M. Pozon

Section
Crown Him King

Special Feature From The

Musical Artist

Known as CIN

Whiskey For The wounded

The Faltering Steps of Kings

Slippery places, slippery places….

Oh how, you have stolen

the sole of the foot kings

They tread upon you lightly

and land amongst the fallen

Your munitions is confusion

and your very spoil

is their faltering steps

The faltering steps of kings

have stepped into bullshit

slid into DMs and ran after lies

The faltering steps of kings

Have walked in their secrets

And waited, just to cheat

They have done everything foolishly

as if wisdom was hid from their eyes

They trod on slippery places

And fall in surprise

J. M. Pozon

"I Ain't Shit."

I ain't shit for real, remember?

You told me that.

So I laughed it off

until you showed me that

No Remorse….

You weren't holding back

But, I loved the idea of you

Infactuated at your beautiful

I'd rather cheat then to leave

So I started playing movie rolls

I lost my conscience

in this scripted vengeance

Fuck it, then!!!

I'm getting even

If you ain't shit?

Then I ain't shit neither

Now we Even…

Whiskey For The wounded

Little Lies

I color myself vibrant

with deceit

Allusive partial truths and

forward speech

A liar confessing lies, is what liars

would never do

But, I cannot tell a lie,

I'm just chopping cherry trues

I'm fine, I'm okay, I'm just tired, and I'm cool.

What's up?

-Shiddd nothin…..

I get it you're a liar too.

Cognac Comforts

Love is long suffering,

That's what the wise all tell me

But, if happiness is made of tears,

I just might see heaven

Eyes the color of Henessy,

I match mix drinks

swith mixed feelings

Pain's the only reminder that I am still living,

But cognac comforts healers

So I'll be sipping as am healing

Whiskey For The wounded

The You, You Hide

I will know the you,

you hide

Your innocence undefiled by societal

conditioning

Your wall of fear, that perverts pride into denial,

will shatter when I kneel before you

Your war with doubt will cease when you

accept the certainty of us

The parallel universe created in the abyss of wonders,

known to your conscientiousness as…

"What if"

Will be torn away from your reality

Simply by the vows we take

The "I do's" I say will be proven by

the "I do's" I show.

And, I will know the "You" you hide

As my glory, my rib, my wife

J. M. Pozon

Made in the USA
Middletown, DE
30 March 2023

27431785R00104